E V E N T S

F I L M

C A N N O T

W I T H S T A N D

EVENTS FILM CANNOT WITHSTAND

. . . . by Zach Savich

**RESCUE
+PRESS**

Rescue Press, Milwaukee 53212

Copyright © 2011 by Zach Savich

Printed in the United States of America

www.rescue-press.org

Cover design by Skye McNeill

Book design by Rescue Press

Photographs by Jeff Downey

First Edition

ISBN: 978-0-9844889-4-0

Library of Congress: 2011922032

for my friends

"Have you practis'd so long to learn to read?"

Contents

One

Two

Three

Four

Five

One

·

·

·

·

The First Swimmer

I want to write you a beautiful book of prose, against not least the before-too-long loss of tongue and sense and all sun-defiant hues on the river bend, and none of us able to say or touch or see, *soon enough, soon enough, aground*, to give you this my voice today nevertheless, withstanding, nevertheless, given everything, for you, a clear note from a complicated bell. I say, *This is how the first swimmer must have felt*. I dreamed you swam out past the rocks and swam out. Windows boarded with the prettiest wood. Pipe organ kinda shadows sloughed off boughs and steeple slant, dear mortal green bandying over a car I saw today patched with a touch of foil.

It is summer and the silver truck for sale down the way has turned blue. My premise is that life and language are larger and livelier than we typically bear, that ideas are only so many words, and life is too short for memoir, and true clarity is not trite but like the light from the first telescope the first swimmer aimed into the interiors of the avidest stars, and weren't we nearly lovers three years before? I imagine you reading because you cannot sleep, because you wish to be interested. And we realize again we know nothing, as ever, yet have lived, well enough, well enough, aground, given everything, *tra la.*

You say I am moving too much but what cannot be said in a sentence.

I cannot be alone in this: for the longest time I have wanted to pen a chronicle of Virgil, having left Dante in purgatory, descending lingeringly back to the underworld. What's not to love, in that scenario? White butterflies among red berries. Three-dimensional shadow of a wire coop. Porch rail roughed, like newsprint on a thumb. A girl kicks against stars on a playground swing. And Virgil—he suffers it, leaving each room as one would an offering, thinking *how can I not be in love, having seen what I've seen?*

And for the longest time this conceit connected to experiments I performed in lucid dreaming, a year I lived in a basement the exact dimensions of my bed. If you wish to fly, for example, I have found it is easiest if you first break a separate physical rule: do not open the window, merely move through its glass. Additionally, suspended bounding is easiest, not swimming in air motions as many maintain. They say the hungriest art students take home the still-life fruit, life models, an entire snowy field at dusk.

Our flaw, of course, is not loving precisely nor distinguishing widely enough. I am speaking about literature and art but mean to do so without specific reference to literature or art, because art and life do not conflict. Often, feelings I have that contradict do not conflict. I can have feelings all day. Every feeling I've ever had has been an epiphany. I consider the willing suspension of disbelief to be, merely, belief, though I have no beliefs to speak of. And have believed too much in suffering, withstanding. Though I can remember speeding our pace to leave the others, directed by strides I do not understand, yet believe for. My mind is mostly things others have said. I have public library pronunciation: I know many words I have never heard.

Here is the hardest thing I know: no matter how good you've been, no matter what you've said or seen or made or been, you are here again bare—hello! Did you know the most misquoted phrase in poetry is Pound's "make it new," which is not really about innovation but continuance? We need to keep making the good. Exist. To make the good insist. In the dark ages Romans forgot their stately aqueducts and turned to drinking river shit. A student recently lectured me blisteringly on a topic I wrote every book about. I do not want to believe too much in suffering or say endurance is all, but. The other day, with the affront and antidote of all real froth, I realized that we do not speak to or as or instead of or of landscape but as a result of it. Consider this a landscape. I do not need to name the trees for you. Latinate.

I am sitting under a tree I can identify if it flowers.

I am not reading but holding the book open waiting for petals to fall for their pressing.

I open the book and call whatever I do reading.

Under a nest held together by the action of feathers moving in it.

I can stare if you are speaking.

One of the most erotic moments, of course, is one feigning sleep drawing a borrowed couch sheet closer so his host may mark his arousal and find herself inclementized. They say Virgil would have seen the emperor's famed fountain making animal shapes with its jets, feathered fins embroidered with sun like tin galloping apart on flat green stones. Have you ever imagined? Virgil may have rinsed an apricot in the hooves of one. I draw the borrowed sheet closer. Here is what I am. Less than a bit of smoke on the horizon scalloped like a yard of oyster shells.

Of course, I like the *Purgatorio* best because it is closest to where we live.

My sadness at the forgotten aqueducts, and resulting plague, is the same sadness I have reading past O'Hara in the anthologies, or the sadness and thrill I had first hearing Hopkins. If such is possible, how can we bear less? We fall, short. So allow me to clearly spear at tangents to suggest the contours (centaurs) of a heart perhaps you are living within. I am thinking of when I was a small-town teen skipping class in my Camaro to find whatever I could at the public library. There are places where desire is enough for you to carry dry topsoil for years in your hands because of the smallest possibility that a seedling is in it or a Camaro.

Push the chairs together to make a train do you see the chairs or the train?

The child wrote *Pencil in a nencil. Pencil, what's a nencil?* I ended class for the day.

I wrote, *The eye is certainly the sexiest thing to look at.* I stood on the train platform, waiting for your eyes, thinking of events film cannot withstand. The first swimmer turned whatever he touched into sea. Did you know I have never seen a fragment?

My heritage, of course, is assimilation, and bootlegging, some fermentation found in every bud. They put my baby grandmother in a dumbwaiter during a knife fight. Her mother fled coal mines. Into a house of ill-standing. And was rescued by the police. Man she came to live with. Perhaps whose brother she married after he came down from Canada. Where he was a letter-writer for others from the country he fled? In a wagon after something with a murder. My heritage is quietness: you should know enough of the language to come across as one who is silent. My heritage: the eventual aphasia and loss of all words we come to soon enough as is, as it is, in spite of all wit and sense and ardor or having sat with hands.

But I could listen to this bird's two notes forever. I could sit here folding blank pages into perfect envelope-size. I will tape the edges and mail them blank. What are you cooking this month? How is it things continue to happen? The only message: I think of you. It is sentimental to say desire fulfilled is loss because I want you here.

One definition: stay in motion.

Of course, we need new terms. And conditions. We need the kind of emergency you have been hoping for, so there can be medicine in this again. Here are events film cannot withstand. The woman's landlord mowing below. She tells me we cannot see each other again because she needs to preserve herself, having come to this edge, we met, and it has marked us, but now, upheld by something we have, given everything, taken from each other, the givens, we come to in our own lives, reminded of, so we yes must separate but there is no hesitation in do we kiss goodbye because we are already. Hills of all I may betray let me not betray the value in this and loving even the ending, spit out new, anew, aground, protectless, faithful only to the rapt sidewalk, swallow, wind on my face so I have a face, junco, the body changing faster than anything like the soul can catch its breath about.

Holyoke Fences

In a strange year in my life I found myself living in Holyoke, Massachusetts, the birthplace of volleyball flushed with defunct mills. Ladders lean out second-level windows, festive deflated inflatables serrate yards, a man shakes his hair dry. Tarp over a skylight. And so many fences I love that run along part of a house then simply stop, keeping nothing out. And fences made from boards merely leaning against wire.

A load of cabbage dumped in an alley on a torqued mattress.

My father said you can put canvas over barbed wire if you ever need to climb it but why would I and if I did would I have canvas or the time to think of it. But I love most his need to teach such. There was an elf in the raspberry bush with a time car.

I want to write you a beautiful book of prose, the kind you will love but find best for carrying, never reading. Yet can you please think of it as the book ever ripe for your bag or for sitting with as though this may be the time finally or you can use it to save a seat? Time and temperature the same on the bank clock. I watched John Wayne movies with the bartender, summer I went out at dusk to exercise my crutches.

We are bound by: wanting to assert, insist, continually prove that this world is enough, is everything we want, if we are willing to want it enough; and wanting to say we can transform it, incite ourselves, find the better ongoing or underlying momentarily hovering through. Yeast is a metaphor and also a fence's paint that looks most like the color you want the instant it comes off the brush. But still how the boards absorb and absorb and the bucket.

I love of course the fences that to go over you may simply walk around.

As I love these lines around my eyes: I feel you could cut a key to match them and it would unlock a door I have been standing before unknowing, perhaps in a flash as a man "struck by lightning on the highway for an hour before somebody stopped to help." In Holyoke I watched a man at the bar with a hand against his forehead I thought first holding his head up drunk but really he was holding a bandage on. The hardware man came in and the mailman. The guitar player asked everyone to move to the far end of the bar to hear.

I honestly once believed disaster was through all only sometimes unmanifest yet. You would be wrong to think I mean anything about substances. I named rock formations: this one is known as Leda of the Rocks. And sought to find them. What is the name of this forest? You know there is a river there by the trees there. You can just walk around each one to reach the river. The emergency exit is only painted on. And the room behind it full of old mattresses.

I spin a bit to find where I am.

What I have found across the country is commonalities of desire we have no name for. The professor asked me my thoughts about the free verse versus formalism debate so I stuttered, but then at dinner later I understood his actual curiosity and hope for everything under. I want you to read this but I want you to read this after you have read every other word I have written. The project is to project. A life projection. Such as insurance agents have been known to misplace and find they must rely instead on extant anecdotes or a very long "party sub."

And while I know my friends will read me I have not fully considered the blunt audience of small children who older will find a shelf their parents collected and forgot for life. I remember when your only word was *Degas*, little Esme, like his reincarnation or one summoning it. We hunted dragonflies on the ebullient yard. Most of what your parents and I have said to each other we have forgotten or would now disagree with so please say. English is a second language. The man we met late the night before left three white fish on a post. Honey wine.

The way around may be through but the way through is then also around, I ventured, and that of course anything I say is actually an expression of a belief (desire) under it, so that when the professor said my work was too experimental and the professor said my work was too traditional each meant really something he or she loved that mine was not though they did not understand I too love what he or she loved—and of course would you trust an artist who did not think of herself as an experimenter traditionalist or did not say art is the reconcilation innovation of the imagination and time which continually expires among our illiteracy? But everything was better in the kitchen much later.

Plastic bags over our shoes to walk to the school bus left in a field. Meant there was snow. Her druggie brother sharpened the Thanksgiving knife wildly.

Another problem is that we do not learn chronologically, we know of Modernism before knowing what it reacted to and also do not understand what we are reading because we learn to understand anything because of the reading, thus the most influential parts of author x to me were features now that do not seem features of author x but of my life in one year I lived for.

And not to mention those who mistake technical effect for historical meaning.

And those who confuse technical expression and the sensibility homesteading there.

And those who don't understand what I mean when I say I have only ever written from not sleeping or a sense that it could save my life, *honestly*, that I understand is not exactly sensible or true but that I trust and desire and try to be accountable to withstanding.

And the altitudes at which air itself becomes hued.

More than the fallacies of populism when we know what real need, desire, empathy, oppression, and censorship breed (the Ardent).

And shiver at those who can afford to say lighten up or act as though none of it matters, nonchalance is a taxidermied pike in the single remaining eye of the world, or who eliminate one or even two thirds of what we have for heart-brains because they lighten up. Where is the verve and the ought? Where is the cinnamon in the snake? Among the small targets many smally hit. While Hopkins called music "faith-heat."

We find ourselves outside the stories. The loss of honor is the loss of pride. I feel myself a threshold. You and I, persistent cockfucks, have gained something we love through unconventional means now to preserve it I find myself wanting to summon conventions which run counter to all I love, much as any avant-garde enters a university's humanist brick. To never become one who from excess of love of one thing does not recognize how that love is present, how that thing exists, in other furnaces, and I would like to be surprised.

You may have known me during the time I studied chronic pain and numbness, having experience of them and believing hewing to such states could render a closer honesty. And then the month I kept a pain notebook and a month later looked back and found it never mentioned pain. But described snow. Your inseam in words. Posthumous, terminal hour I preferred certain crosswalks at. To be connoisseur of nothing you can see. I love the moment of stutter most: speaking in the mosaic room, how I felt obliged to say beyond the limit of what I can easily say, the world's oldest teenager, how the many square tiles come to a curve, your posture better in a field or the dark.

No—the stutter that goes on, not merely sound of fingers ethereal on strings or the breathing of the singer haunting the tape, we are not so weary and broken that merely any present voice will do, nor silence, but want the stutter and the going on with the aid of eyebrow or you can touch my neck, as clapping can keep time for a breaking voice, behold now the mosaic from a distance up to one mile. This cut will not heal without staples.

She said a perfect radio could find Moses in air. Then, as a match loosed down a well achieves its most telling sense by going dark, she closed her eyes.

The point of studying landscape is you then realize everything is landscape as the point of staring into eyes was to then see anything as it was looking back, much as when you realize you have been quoting something you've never read or someone indicates there's a bit of lemon in the stew. I saw the lichens then everything in relation to. Blossomed where paintballs primed the bigbox stores.

The moment still life painting shifted to accommodate pouring wine, a spun coin, candle flame, the entire snowy field at dusk. Do you have the time?

More and more, I appreciate the stone tower's clock that strikes once for half past and doesn't bother with the hours. Even what doesn't repeat is a pattern. You can recognize the horizon because you are standing there. Remember when we lived at the sea?

A Holyoke fence, then, is anything you believe obstructs until you find you are examining it from every angle to figure out how to get through it and see you have already gone around. I have been trying not to quote but find myself thinking of Roethke, since I have never not been in love:

> *What lover keeps his song*
>
> *I sigh before I sing*
>
> *I love because I am*
>
> *A rapt thing with a name*

You know I rely too much on memory so cannot tell you how the punctuation goes or if I have ever read those lines before. How about a little more life in your life? Could you go for some right now? Also: there is no Hell, only your body, and the pre-emptive necrophilia that true love is. Think of a tin can phone and you are the string between them.

Blurb

Here is the history of song:

    1. *La la la*

    2. *La la la mother*

    3. *Mother mother mother*

So they asked me to write my own sentences about my second book of poetry and I tried some smooth uprightness against the roughness I trust:

"Unafraid of emotion and innovation, Zach Savich's *Annulments* passionately expands and deepens love poetry for the new century. Its major poem, 'The Mountains Overhead,' draws from Dante,

Whitman, H.D., and soul music to offer a singular coming-of-age story of geography and affection. Just one year after Savich's debut collection introduced readers to his ardent intelligence and uniquely dexterous faith in music and the world, *Annulments* affirms this young poet's extraordinary range and capacious, wild elegance. Mingling epistle and proverb, classicism and experiment, *Annulments* daringly journeys through the heart's truths and their consequences. With the confidence of a troubadour, it proves that when things break apart, they can break into song."

To act as though we are what we may be. But saving nothing, excess will make up the balance.

If excess burns off what is the fire?

You may write to get something out of your system but then you are a system.

In Chicago we learned the municipal device is a symbol is a Y representing the river, you can see it hidden among architecture or public works. I believe the municipal device of Lincoln, Nebraska, where I circled the drain happily for some cloud-colored days, should be the Etruscan wall painting D.H. Lawrence describes and that I saw in its earthen mound of no hell. It is an image but also a metaphor in which there are three figures, which and how many are you: a man holding a leash; a man whose neck is held by the leash, bag over his head and a club in his hand; a dog that is trying to gnaw up the bag-headed man's crotch. You see, it looks like torture, as Lawrence or Freud would explain, but is actually a game which is actually civilization—the man tries to club the dog to death before the dog can eat the man's junk. It is a game because of the leash, which functions as a line in poetry ought. To write in free verse you might say is like playing this crotch-dog game without a leash around your neck?

Lineage, we say: the age of one's line.

But every sentence now is about the latest book less certainly.

So I have decided to provide a line by line annotation of the beginning of the central poem from the aforementioned book, *Annulments*. I will provide it but not the source material that sparked it, rather perhaps a deeper source material the sparking returns me to. You should know that I wrote this poem in a matter of months. I saw it as an exorcism, having left a relationship at 21 to go to poetry school and feeling therefore my poems had to match in value the person I had left, foolishly thought and impossible—for writing to equal a person, to make that leaving come out right— but also prodded me well. I wrote the poem to sew the staple of loss up in. It also contains every good line I wrote before writing this poem, the uneroding lines from poems that were not worth saving, from days I learned to write by wandering tonally or by logic from a killer first line to a killer last one, microwave dings we're done, but why not have every line be a first and last line?

I lived in a white room with snow outside and a very small desk in a little nook by a white chair. I hadn't read anything yet. I hadn't yet lived in Paris, hadn't gone to New Zealand. The sections in the poem are numbered so my explanations are, too. You understand that I want to give the kind of explaining you do not give in workshop or when your book is merely read. And to be part of the sense that all we ever do is revise the same ideas, the same impulses, every book a first book, every book we may write the same book, every book we will ever write merely a version of *Leaves of Grass* and *Of Being Numerous*.

Consider me a translation. Consider me one who finds half of what he sees tied to things he has read or written before, hoping to find that while we—make it new—keep making the good exist, we need to find what bears repeating. Because—how was your day?—repeating bears us. We are made of repetitions but not all repetitions are worth making (bare).

The title was first *Song* then my teacher said a slight alteration would improve it (my teacher was Cole Swensen; I turned in and found the final form for this long poem in a class she taught on long poems that Kiki Petrosino, Robert Fernandez, Kristin Hatch, Andy Stallings, John Craun, and other friends were also in; she told me which syllables were off; my other teacher read it and said it was "vaguely about love but love's not vague" and I heard only the comment's pentameter) so I called it *Sung* which it was as a whole on its own that was almost published several times but probably seemed too spaced out like a white futon in a white room. The whole thing is full of notes I could not hit now or would not but that I am glad exist, shards of bell. This was. A time I believed in sentiment and felt sight inseparable from music, perception itself a kind of line and my neck leashed fine. But now the title is *The Mountains Overhead* which is clouds of course or an idea of heaven or more accurately flight, and brings Dante to mind and is a quote from Yeats on a similar subject of early and lost love and art. Here is the rest of what I am for you, my correspondences:

1.

I did not know what this phrase meant but felt it as meaningful or rather significant and the meaning will become clear in the end as most revealed things. On the radio they spoke of the prophecy that at last made sense in 1988 though today it does not again.

2.

This event is present in many cultures and literature, I have found over time, but really was a recording of something that happened to me in the white room above. And you quickly realize any line sung becomes an entire world, as a singer can say *oh* and we shiver for this. I love refrain, meaning burden, in its archaic term, what one carries, it carries, carries one. Do we dream in song or only in iambic pentameter? You are reading a book in a dream but what were the words. You must believe if you could only remember it would be the most astonishing life sentence.

The cygnets are on a postcard, which is on my white door. Tape pulls off paint, a visual echo of the end of a reel of audio tape.

3.

I have been told that augurs were veiled so they would not accidentally read an omen in incidentals and be forced to give the emperor knowledge he would be better served not to know. For example, when we have already decided to battle. It is wrong to know the outcome if that outcome will be. Wrong meaning honor.

To make sense means to make sensation, says James Merrill. And we know this is true, because we have lives of sensation, but also sad because the sense we think of when we "make sense" cannot touch us, for example in a musical situation such as "please see for me she has a coat so warm."

4.

The birds were real, called *laser tag* in earlier poems. I saw many grey dawns. And couldn't sleep for wishing I would wake in another year entirely, as in the poem by Apollinaire. I couldn't sleep alternately because of the hope and impossibility of such beamed-away waking, how sensational hope and impossiblity were and real. Could leave your apartment and be in any city.

5.

The truest thing I know. Why write a book except to dedicate it? The truest book would be all dedication or text in which the text was indistinguishable from the dedication. You may read every line I write as a dedication. Go to the lecture so we may leave together early. That pleasure the first time it happened under sycamores planted for the dead students of WWI, after and better than the pleasure of being at the first lecture after-party like we were at.

6.

It is important to imagine actual paradise. Fences for only our own dogs. In the summer I lived with a woman because my leg was broken I studied mining, remembering towns I had driven through in Idaho. Our country young enough to have been shaped by industries of a moment already passing but shapes remain. The cream curdled from the coffee's heat, shadows of power lines thick enough to bump a pick-up. Scree straight into the screen door of the back porch. You are home.

7.

The woman I lived with when I had a broken leg and I borrowed a friend's car and drove to a lake half an hour away. A summer of Sam Cooke. The mountain is probably Rainier but not in any way I can be sure of. May be the one Pound mentions in his *Pisan Cantos*. No I think now it is not any mountain I have ever seen that is why it cannot be concealed—can't hide what you can't find yet know is closer than here now will be.

8.

As a child of course you investigate the droppings of things and if you are lucky can break them open and see what was. The owl is especially intriguing because noctural and its eyes and noise but you know also belongs to Athena, it is her municipal device and what she had instead of a cell phone.

9.

Traces left meaning there is movement still or up ahead.

10.

In love space of course famously changes to the span of one's hand
or the distance elbow to waist you know in your sleep, so time also
changes, becoming un-relative.

11.

You have faith that there is always a rhyme for something or
potential pun for example if you pronounce it correctly the
name of any town can become the name of a famous painter,
language's supple capacity is endless, you must believe, so the
false etymology and associations are more true, they are ten-thirds
of what we speak, every word actually sandwiched among these
others we feel in ways that are not random but also you cannot
rationalize. And then other faiths that are learned: I see "bow"
and think of Keats' last letter, naturally, forever now.

Every line amounts to the same, to continually learn a certain
present. This this how. Vow now how. To whatever extent you will.

A man charging into battle crying *I have...*

[There are one hundred and eight more sections, but why respond
to them when everything is response—that is, what I transmit

here is the responding, which is in the clock and faucet in this apartment keeping adjacent headings, or the phrase from reading Lincoln's collected prose this morning that has stuck with me, "sufficiently abundant," his description of a year's harvest, or a cadence in my head from Alice Notley, which I wish to adapt into the sentence "you may say after great pain a formal feeling comes, but then you are Emily Dickinson," or last night leaving the sushi restaurant near the Sycamore Mall not knowing for a moment which way was town or north and then the gradual dawning, which some day will no longer dawn, of sense, as I will sometimes call the library at the school where I am now by the name of the library at the other school where I was, the brain's capacity (for association/relation/sorting strangely past sense libraries together with words) also its downfall, we will all come untongued soon enough as is—and also once a sequence, a procedure, has been established, why would you need to carry it out? As soon as I know what I am doing I cannot. So most essays I write become a sentence. Proved it so thoroughly I don't need to again. Would rather entitle.

Don't you find sentences becoming? If I was your sentence I'd be coming too—that's one joke my new love interest and I often make. Also, after many phrases: "how'd you know my high school nickname?" The grains of sand are not beach but desert unless you also make a sea, which is made by swimming. It is the only way to measure the sea, those gathering strokes. Last night at dinner someone described a pond dyed blue at a complex in Des Moines. It is partly aesthetic—to make the water more clearly (bluely) water—but also did you know it prevents algae from forming by changing what water is? Water can be more purely water (less algae) by becoming something other than natural, thus purity may be by proportion or definition. I believe all of this relates, but I wish we were speaking, because then we could decide to lie down.

I like you because you run ahead of what I am saying and see where I am going, which means you can counter this. Hello. I like the dog because he mistakes the large truck side passing for actually being the ground, which he loves to run along impossibly near his nose never however skinned. Saving some pee.

There are one hundred and eight more sections, but don't you find suggestion enough? It is hard to write a sonnet that surpasses ababcdcdefefgg.

And have you, a reader, ever read W.H. Auden's second book, *The Orators*? I came across it while reading all of Auden the other day. It is the strangest book I know, not least because he wrote it. You could compare it to Lou Reed's *Metal Machine Music*, but that would not contend with how it shows Auden as he always was. The best way to describe it is to have you find a picture of Auden's face when he is old. His face is incomprehensible (comprehensive), flappy and huge, a palm tree growing out of an overstuffed sofa at sunset. *The Orators* is what he wrote when he was young that looks exactly like his aged face. It is disturbing in what it does and calls a book, not because it is conceptual but because it is actual. My favorite concept is the actual.

How strange it all is, having a body, which language cannot fix yet may clarify, so we find after researching chronic pain that nearly everyone has some sort of chronic pain. As in turtlenecks. Remember when you realized that it didn't matter if anyone read your diary, because all of our secrets are the same? Sometimes I worry that I "love life too much." I don't know anyone whose life is like mine, not counting everyone. Remember when you stopped noticing the bugs and realized it meant you had stopped noticing yourself?

My father taught me: you don't need to disarm the bomb until it is at 3 or 2 or 1. I would like that sentence read whenever anyone thinks of me. Thus, should you wish to disarm the bomb you should ask how may I speed the clock.

The brain is wallpapered. This wallpaper used to be somebody's dress. Notice the tears you can see under. It looks different than in the catalog. And a mobile of many shiny teeth. And because of reading Lincoln this morning now I see "sufficient abundancy," "sufficiently abundant," everywhere. There is a way of making coffee that exercises the muscles you need for flying a kite and a way of making coffee so you will have something to write a poem about.

To ever ask: what is the underlying impulse. Tell me the difference between nostalgia and the recognition of fate. Has anything ever been an interruption or an example of further continuity? What isn't nonfiction.]

While I was learning to write poems it was popular to use words like *bevel, cobalt*, and *the cartography of*. For a time in the 1980s innovative fiction loved quantum physics, emotional corrollaries to the behavior of electrons etc. Now, after captivity narratives, phantom limbs, and ekphrasis, there is neuroscience, loved also for how it breaks mystery but has a veneer. For example I have read about infantile consciousness. It resembles poetic states—can't accurately sort cause and effect in sequence; can't predict that what is current (like a feeling) won't be forever; can't tell that others can't feel what you do.

This is tied to infants not having a continuous self in time via language—so poets employ language to capture states in which we don't have enough or refined language? More interesting, though, is that the process of continuous self in time via language begins at age 5 and ends (one afternoon) in your early 20s. Which clearly explains the popularity of creative writing classes for undergraduates, function of such classes, general early lyricism—to return in a sophisticated way, at the close of one arc of language/self/time integration, to the beginning of that arc, to disintegration which is also now sensible, uninfantile. I wish to always trail off and have you chime in now.

With luck such neuro-inquiry in poetics will surpass the interest in ekphrasis which at its unsophisticated is a form of interspecies kleptoparasitism rather than a mode of looking which as Cole says may be applied anywhere, art a continuous start. Let me see the self or your shoes as I would a veneer. I mean a Van Gogh.

Remember when I suddenly could not stand Impressionism, the solipsism of the eye's alterations in light? And now can regard Monet one day a month.

If poetry is "original research in language" (Pound) what is language and does he mean we are researching within language, advancing the research of language, or researching something else (life) and language is the means.

If poetry is "original research in language" of course original means origins and remember when our friend (you told me) pronounced original with the wrong emphasis and vowel sound, or-i-GINE-ul? New origins lying in the.

If poetry is "original research in language" how do we get *in* language.

It is a cliché but important to at some point hear someone say do I speak language or does language speak me. Then to say do such questions as do I speak language or does it speak me speak me.

The final line can change your life though you resist such summation.

Must I change my life or change with it, like owls?

Have I wasted my life or wasted with it, much as the mule elk?

There is the impulse toward disappearing, as Basho's attempted suicide by journeying. To write a book that cannot be read but tastes, as in to name a book with the title of an existing book that will always come up first, or be published by the ocean. The jokes that only your friends get but you have no idea who your friends are unless you start joking. I tried to explain to the stand-up comedian that he mostly referred to things people already agree are funny, but he told me about the eternal and I laughed.

For a while a few of us tried to write a book called *500 Feelings You Should Be Having* and were in a band.

One day a few of us wrote the book *Delicious Willows* as a study in the sounds of r and l and it was published by river? / fox press. During a tough hour in its composition, Jeff Downey extracted a huge stone from the center of a path. It is known as the bleedstone, as in what you need when you are bleeding, rather than a bandage. The best poem in the book is a single line.

River Horses

I butterflied into and then away from one.

These are inside jokes but I would like you to come in. You should see my outside jokes. Remember the Berryman poem that goes *Love me love me love me love me love me*? Or when Nico and Comstock wrote the poem *I am the first lady / of fuck you. / My interests are education, health care, / and fuck you.* There are no photographs of the most famous ballerinas.

My father taught me: you don't need to disarm the bomb until it is at 3 or 2 or 1. Should it have a fuse not a timer you must count down yourself starting with 100.

All Extant If

The answer to failed love: more love.

The answer to did you come: about toward.

The answer to despair: croissant-wich.

Here is an existing appetite.

Instructions printed on the food.

Other dusks one walked softly with.

My lover washing.

My lover opening a compact mirror.

This fountain they box in winter so no snow mars its jets.

Behind the house: a barn much larger than the house.

Windows open like a letter.

As all things made an example of.

Shutters open like a shirt.

You have been carrying a letter in your shirt.

So in every epic there is the island where nothing happens.

So through my white t-shirt: chest hair appears like a hole.

The smell of the bandage: smells from within a bandage.

Nothing depends.

You are the world's oldest teenager.

Therefore, "to start again with something beautiful" (Plumly).

I am writing this on Walt Whitman's birthday in 2010, 27 years old.

Yeast is a metaphor.

The only way to look into is to look around.

And the music Marsyas played after the god flayed him.

Must sound like clover.

To *debouche* a martial term for coming into the open, from the mouth.

And then we may *rebouche*, returning to one's mouth.

I stare at the mouth while it speaks as though sound or I am there (mirror).

English is a second language.

I have never seen anything that is not clear—to look into it, through.

Go ahead.

Ointments.

This man has made his house a store: only nothing's for sale.

This looks like a bruise: but is a scar.

Here is a skeleton small enough to wear on your hat: or save a seat.

To not be paralyzed, knowing all the reasons one should.

To solve for nothing.

To give a further part of the sequence which all preceding may reveal itself in light of.

To be in light of.

And understand for many god is not a metaphor.

That metaphor is indistinguishable from perception, in any case.

I mean realism.

The matter of manners.

Too happy to read, at least once a day, but I stare out, as in, into, through, or around.

One who worked as a house painter.

Painted the sights of his lost home.

On all the new interiors.

Upon returning home.

Painted every flower and menu item white.

They are painting the stems of tulips blue in Old La Paz.

Easy now.

I like what makes me un.

May break apart upon re-entry.

The opposite of Icarus: unbearably buoyant.

They would not allow the first swimmer to come ashore for hours.

Unsure of the effects.

There used to be other strokes than we know: one called painting the stems.

One called making you coffee without waking you.

I wouldn't trust the one who believes me.

Or thinks I look interesting because I sit here writing.

But of course: we love too much.

Rapt nothing in this light we cannot see.

Sensibility Quizz

Honestly answer:

1. Which do you prefer salve, salvage, or salvation?

2. A man becomes a monster or a monster becomes a man?

3. I want to be alone but I want your body or I want your body but I want to be alone?

4. At which point do you no longer thoroughly hear the phrase "you can have your cake and eat it too":

    a) you can have my beefsteak and sleep too

    b) you can take a walk around the block and come back home too

    c) you can to

5. Given the title of this section, do you think the extra "z" is:

    a) my bad

    b) hinting that the title truncates a longer phrase such as "sensibility quizzes" in which "quiz" is a verb

6. What's the most influential book for your life you will never read?

7. Would you rather be struck, arrested, touched, or moved?

8. To make this room brighter will you:

a) turn on the light

b) turn off all the other rooms' lights

9. Like how some sea animals have dark backs so predators above looking down see only depths, would you like to have a darker back?

10. Watermelon or watertowers?

11. It is time to go or there is time to go?

Two

The Flag You Will Plant On
The Peak Is A Blindfold Before

The relationship as research into relationship. Where there's smoke, there's mirrors: today in the park before I discovered the antique stone stairway leading to log cabins, everyone paused for the anthem piped with many cymbal splashes from the baseball fields. If you go along the river far enough you will cross it, though it's best to imagine you are farther west. Does the heart set more like a bone or the sun? If the heart stops you may stay alive briefly by moving your body as a heart around it.

Dim enough, the lamps may serve as decorative. The only pick-up line: *wanna*? Today near the park I watched a horse nuzzling a fence the next storm will break (the next storm only softens the post). You know there are those for whom the shape of a chair means more than if we need a chair (as though to speak authoritatively of shades, though it will shadow one's authority). Turning for the most beautiful at each intersection will not necessarily lead you to the most beautiful yet will lead you.

To step out now like a belt through its loops, coffee through old grounds, culverts, culverts, the bougainvillea (as clapping can keep time for a breaking voice, before dissembling into confused applause). I could not tell the water in the rowboat from her oiled hair, the man rowing with a top hat from one in recline, needle scar on inner elbow fold like the last dot of espresso in its cup. Today what's the park (one walking can touch what he can't mend). Still, the shadows of the human figure (sketched) seem soft as from an insurmountable watering can. Your look tastes my temperature?

The research is in relation, keen isolation of late afternoon in the quiet trilling tall grasses, so sun leads us wider through the charged. Now people do not make poems but landscape. Now people are writing poems with characters in them but a character is only a type of refrain. I'd like the coffee that is as big as my head but of course my head becomes the size of whatever cup. Mug up like a telescopic lens, everything always coincident, not making me better but taking me better. This is nothing but a specific kind of nothing.

What seemed longing was mourning and moving past. A girl talking to her mother from anywhere in the house, fingers black from all day with the basil, tomatoes suspended in a basin. Walking home near dawn Steve put his face to the sidewalk to see his dream better. Later a boy asked me if an hourglass would burst during flight. It's possible to have ideas all day, or find the one idea you are having is of having ideas all day. My regimen was to sweat by any means or number (as though care changes pain to suffering).

When I say I want all the tires to go flat with you I mean to handle it. The goats were loose on the dirt road home, near the salmonberries. If your ears weren't red when you got to school in the morning it meant you'd got a ride so someone would box them to redden. With the shovel near the carrot beds I did not care to dig to "China" but was interested in constructing a squared hole. We thought we were writing poems but really were writing research re: gender. You cannot tickle yourself.

Are things worse than before or worse because of before (I wanted to be implicated more, warming my hands, occasionally, in fists). They did not cut down the trees around Emily's house for money, as I supposed, but for historical accuracy. But once you care to imagine you see clouds she would have (today on the radio I heard that no one will live forever). I stand here to give you more privacy (distance) but find I now stare directly toward. Glass famous for if you kiss or touch it all remains clear.

Three

Intertitles

Daily and Sunday

They call this newspaper an *obituary source.*

Instructions

To make something new exist just move faster or slower than everything that already exists.

Autobio

Childhood: it rained.

Also Autobio

Childhood: I stayed in bed playing Spot the Similarities with unrelated photographs.

Crotch and Vine

The man without legs held out a rose he was selling like roses were manufactured from his legs.

On Alberti

The handle of the cart is not strictly speaking curved but is worn down by hand enough to be curved.

Paygrade: Waitlist

Why did you bring me to this restaurant she says he says I built it for you. "I can be interested only in things I cannot invent" (Valéry).

Prospectors Return to the Outfitters' Saloons

A building's shadow touches a building, or two buildings' shadows meet on a third.

Echolalala

One way to see what you have written is to read everything else that has been written, then, as by sketching air around a table, deduce.

The Coercive Second Person

There are not enough second persons in our language.

Parade Route

I paint bird silhouettes on everything as though everything is clear.

In Your Eyes!

Why is this ballet you have brought me to so astonishing she said he said it is because the dancers stay in place as the floor moves up and down with varying speeds, in varying sections, depending on your eyes.

Lullaby

Lullaby: *you wanna race my pulse? you wanna close my eyes?*

What Has Made You a Wolf Has Made You

While we have mastered sky writing we still struggle with wild wolf writing.

No Comment

The ground is right where I left it.

My Satisfaction with the Seasons

I applaud to find where the stage is.

Seasonable in Every Season

Sally the mannequin is a flotation device like your breasts are when I am holding them over the water.

After Chaplin

If you fail as a waiter the restaurant may hire you as a singer.

To be by desire "shot through" was less an arrow's discrete path than the expanding systems of rough-shot spreading through in drift from an original point of entry. Given prevailing winds,

and "gestures of invincible desire," to be assailed by longing may liken to being sailed by it, as some sail by winds, some by the consternating stars.

If love is car I am the snowbank, say, you took the autumn behind my eyes and shaped a leafy city there. I found a fine shoe in curb snow I wanted to bring you, wanted more to give you this which was very precise to me but so are you already so by the properties of reason I give you nothing. But how about how a threshold, neared, warms and divides, or you may lift your center to make jut what I lap at.

Dear. The name I thought was a blossom was a river. The child's map included geese, he called them swans. It included every needle of the pine.

Aubade

Dawn: I find your image in the developing room.

Pillowslip

She said are any of them real or only all of them.

Also Aubade

He said there is this way of running your hand up a stem to make a flower-shape of leaves in your palm. You can see it for a moment when you open your palm.

To close your eyes at bliss or the hope for it, in no version do you know you are wishing by to be by this passionate nature contented for further passional contention. Margins became origins,

a virginalia one might hope to "take" a lover to. As any thought absent passion could as well be any other while any with it was it only. In "to wish to be" you can't say

which verb is the infinitive, though you said it has to happen and I understood it has to happen next. To winch upbraid, I mean, to winch upbright, upright a turned trunk felled by its fruits' weight one had to hoist this by his entire house's siding.

It is different being cold if one is in theory solely passing through, though more different to undress an assumption for example your recipient's ability to after opening an envelope see a sunset to the letter.

Four

·

·

·

·

I Remember Your Hand Eyes
Because The Year Was

Sometimes I catch myself remembering, as one stumbling can catch himself running. I remember looking for a house wishing I was looking for a piazza at noon. Posthumous hour. There are some dogs in the splendid marble fountain. No, they built this marble fountain around the dogs. Yes, the dogs are marble.

In my memory I speak to you the way one crosses the busy intersections in the ancient capital: the traffic adapts around you, never lessening its speed but forming more or less lanes, leaning. If you maintain a steady pace and angle, you will be fine. Much in this way don't you think language adapts as we enter, unsure if anything known constantly is also memory.

Everybody thinks. Andy said, *To speak about the world although it ends*. One reason you need to keep writing is you can't bear to read over what you have written. I traded my camera for binoculars and ascended. It is structural—you have been me exactly or will be. It is impossible to read any word and not if comprehending believe. The question is not of technique or association but what you believe you must remain accountable to.

To think at once: there is nothing but the others who have preceded me and thought/lived hotter than I have but it is gone; there is nothing but this woman this window. Do not ask me what I have dreamed. I love imagining the homesteaders here wading together or the precision and roughness of dynamiting ice from the river.

Thunderman's Folly

As long as one wall of the original structure remains you are permitted to build anything with the original building permit. But Greg Thunderman left only a single post, and now can't get another permit: the field is a floodplain. Don't you love our recent history, that we don't know what a floodplain is. They built this entire city out of one year's harvest.

We balance mast-standing-like on the post, Thunderman's Folly. Discuss what one post remains that does not permit the original permit yet substantiates what was. I bring my new lover two apples and a stone. This is not a year for flowers, meaning they are already our element, don't need augmented, flowers of the very air. If only one of my words remains.

Day clear as a thick glass ashtray. Day made worse. And all I remember from the lanugage is *is it possible to have.* Then gesture with the neck. Elsewhere I have described. I have explained it so thoroughly I no longer recall. The birdfeeder is a transparent cylinder. The cat unlatches. Ceiling fans. Am I frivolous. Most ideas I can talk about or "follow" but would never have.

Though was happy at the café to contribute to the thought: when we speak of a technical effect in writing it is not perceived as we mean. For example, the metaphor of the "camera" in realist fiction. Does not come from screenwriting style "long gravel drive seen over plaid lady's shoulder" but more from prepositions. Or you could have anyone identify which kind of light a poem corresponds with. Not by the poems mentioning light but by a word like "politely." That was a fun idea to have.

Compensatory Damages

Oh, but I think grace is reckless. It is the opposite of smallness. And woke this morning to a hummingbird in the miniblinds.

I don't mind. I have heard to catch a bat you can toss up an empty coffee can and it will dive into the turning darkness as it falls. I don't think a hummingbird would have any interest in that, unless it believed some nectar were inside, perhaps sweeter for the turning if not for this darkness.

I want to see people but fear I only want to see people because I am lonely, and is that fair to the people, and also the obviousness of my gratitude and fondness will surely make me insufferable or lead to further loneliness on parting. They are merely blocks away. They have replaced tombstones at the cemetery with inscribed bowls you may take one. No, those are satellite dishes.

The sky close as a policeman's shoulder. I don't mind. What appetite might I walk out for now?

***

"Anyway. Please don't take the above as anything other than thoughts I wish to have with you. Wanting the motions of energy to be constant and now I find myself alone in a house and— you move to read or write and then what? and then the bad thoughts of what's the difference then of having written/read or not, if all is a kind of coping with time? which of course all in a way is but that's not any kind of attitude or else is but is Beckett— the other text I want to read but haven't is Wm. James' 'Radical Empiricism' mostly for the phrase but also for my sympathy with (as ever, but in more complicated ways now) feeling like memory and knowledge don't influence as much as adapt around the present, not so that ideas don't exist as I have before felt but so that their meaning (type of existing) is like traffic on a busy street that stops or keeps going faster or separates suddenly into three lanes as you cross.

"I like you. Light rain this morning. Thunder flashes last night while I played the video game, sick of reading. Would that be a good name for a video game?"

The Life Experiment: Thick Patched Metal Of An Old Truck

This morning I read an essay by someone smart advocating for what amounts to death of a sort, not death but the extinguishing of all desire and roughness I trust, among these ill-soldered hills, faith that nothing that repeats is also a pattern, faith that we need what passes the insufficient official tongues we could never live or talk. My friends make my grumpiness irrelevant, by how they talk and live and tease me out of thought. But I don't understand why so many fear the. Said behind the hand. I'm just. The clarity I want a city within this city I have never seen, where you look at the wires among ivy and there is no conflict between finding this world enough and seeing it transform. Clarity means "luminous." Clarity means "to low." Not can art matter but art is matter. Not make it new but makes us anew.

If we had a temple, these birds would be its frontier. If wind enters through the screen, we removed our shirts. The boat formed around a single bit of leaf. Given this tremendous sail, who alive will mind the smallness of our boat?

Five

.

.

.

.

There Will Be Medicine In This Again

---

too 3d   hard pears on the roof   green and tin

near a blue mailbox

little lion puppets scramble from

bride's dress we named   "dented sedan pristine around its tank"

the apocalypse is younger than us

in spring the silver truck turns white   my lover's parts

like cigarettes lit on a stove

I prefer scarves out of sleeves

for seasickness they say stare at a fixed

point on the horizon   but then homesickness

calendar attempt

we woke to pigeons moaning in the fire escape

dogwood and the scent of rain   dogwood its pink drill treads

alarmed in rain think

of brick where another building was pulled away looking

lightly touched by sun

sun defiant

I can pronounce instantly so it sounds like on the other hand

tobacco guesses

can't our solution be   it's not a problem

the earliest plant you know   helicopter seeds

children employed in naming paintings

so what sun stubbles the player piano keys

whenever I pause   I hear

aubade

to leave each room as you will an offering   boxwood

brick painted white tinting pink over us

crotch and vine

dandelion stems shade the whole path pink

understand I have written everything this year within reach of her

her wallpaper   used to be somebody's dress   violets now

not the purple we have always known but white hued

darker from a purple center

where there's smoke there's mirrors

"in the 1790s there was the isolation of air

scientists breathed carbon monoxide   until their throats blued

and flowers died about them   they did not find

the breath to cure tuberculosis   but nitrous oxide

one noted this could ease the pain of surgery

yet laughing gas was not used clinically for forty years"

this morning in the west

yellow flowers no one ever named

in scrap wind   near mule elk in a copse

there will be medicine in this again

every board here boarded   some view up

ditch shimmer   enough has happened

this year I don't care

if anything does

action of finches   up air, back

fence, along   in praise of consequences

and bulky weathered bales

Zach Savich is the author of three books of poetry, *Full Catastrophe Living*, *Annulments*, and *The Firestorm*, as well as the chapbook *The Man Who Lost His Head*. He was born in Michigan.

RESCUE
+PRESS